YOUR KNOWLEDGE HAS VALUE

Strategic and System Thinking. Practice of a Strategy

Sixbert Sangwa

Bibliographic information published by the German National Library:

The German National Library lists this publication in the National Bibliography; detailed bibliographic data are available on the Internet at http://dnb.dnb.de.

ISBN: 9783346416858
This book is also available as an ebook.

© GRIN Publishing GmbH
Nymphenburger Straße 86
80636 München

Print and binding: Books on Demand GmbH, Norderstedt, Germany
Printed on acid-free paper from responsible sources.

The present work has been carefully prepared. Nevertheless, authors and publishers do not incur liability for the correctness of information, notes, links and advice as well as any printing errors.

GRIN web shop: https://www.grin.com/document/1014892

Critical Evaluation of Stacey's Statement: *"Systems thinking essentially seeks to understand phenomena as a whole formed by the interaction of parts"* (Stacey, 2011)

Sixbert Sangwa

MBA Student at University of South Wales

September 2017

Abstract: This essay serves as a critically appraise the above statement *"Systems thinking essentially seeks to understand phenomena as a whole formed by the interaction of parts"* (Stacey, 2011) in relation to changing ideas of strategic thinking and explain how it exists within the author's business approach to strategic management. The key themes addressed consist of an analysis of approaches to Strategic Thinking, Systems Thinking, Complexity Perspective, especially the New Ways of Thinking about Strategy, Complex Adaptive Systems, especially Modelling Complexity, and The Practice Perspective.

Keyword: Strategic Systems Thinking, Strategic Tools, Linear thinking, Systems thinking, Strategy, Synergy.

Index

1. Introduction

Today's business environment is Complex, Dynamic, multi-faceted and the environment has a far- reaching impact. As for other organizations, the author's company's environment is a combination of several factors that surround and affect it. Therefore, the management of such environment requires managers to carry out a careful analysis of the entire environment to have a clear understanding on how to position the firm in the industry based on fitting the strategy to the current business environment. The implication is that business managers should scan both internal and external environment in order to adopt /develop strategies that they think will make their businesses successful.

According to Ndaruhutse, Jones, & Riggall (2016): one of the biggest breakthroughs in how we understand and guide change in our organizations is systems theory and systems thinking. System thinking and strategic thinking are two interrelated terms that deal with examining patterns and lead to decision making and the planning for execution at the organizational level. To understand how both strategic and system thinking are used in organizations, we will clearly define what systems are. To be able to evaluate strategic system thinking and systems tools in our organization, we need to explicitly define both strategies and systems. This will also lead us to the analysis on complexity of organizational system.

1.1. Strategy

According to Caves and Ghemawat (1984), a strategy is a contingent *plan of action* designed to achieve a particular goal.

Similarly, Porter (1996) defines strategy as "*the creation of a unique and valuable position, involving a different set of activities.*"

Johnson Scholes (2011) defines a corporate strategy as "*the direction and scope of an organisation over the long term which achieves advantage for the organisation through its configuration of resources within a changing environment to meet the needs of markets and to fulfill stakeholder expectations*"

In all cases, strategy refers to the creation of approaches/actions that a firm has to undertake in order to minimize the external threats and internal weakness, maximize the external opportunities while increasing internal strength; putting emphasize on the organization visions.

1.2. Intended/deliberate and emergent strategy

Johnson, Whittington and Scholes (2011) explain the difference between the two types of strategy as based on strategy development. Deliberate strategy which he describes as the rational or analytic view of strategy development, is developed based on some tools, techniques and frameworks for strategic analysis and evaluation (Johnson, 2011). On the other hand, emergent strategy is not developed based on long-term planning and often emerge when deliberate strategies have gone bad.

2. Strategic thinking

Strategic thinking merely refers to the thinking about the strategy (Wilson, 1994). Leonidas (2011) argues that *"Strategic thinking entails thinking regarding the purpose, values, along with processes and individuals and other resources"*. *"It is a means of perceiving the sphere based on the bigger picture, the basic patterns, the prospect, as well as based on the setting or context"* Added Leonidas. Feyzollah and Saeid (2015) argue that the process deals with the in-depth analysis of the opportunities and problems as well as the impact of company's action on other actors. It refers to thinking on the long-term vision and planning for the implementation of long-term strategy at the organizational level.

Strategic thinking is the approach in which business leaders think and creates the future for their organization. It looks beyond today and anticipates long-term problems, opportunities, and new realities. This proactive process focuses on how to create an organizational vision by scanning business environment and adopting required changes, and often, profound personal change. *"It refers to proactively planning for the results your business would achieve in the future and creating an ideal future by defining and achieving results that adds values to the company. Strategy, in business, is the combination of foresight, planning, and decision-making that prepares an enterprise to achieve long-term goals and manage the consequences of contemporary decisions"*

(Saad A, 2013). Hence, creating a strategy implies deciding on both the actual and long-term objectives of an organization.

3. System thinking

Reisman, R. and Oral, M. (2005) define the system thinking as it is tidy thinking and observing the causal relation between the operation factors through the working medium. While Leonidas S (2011), described all organizations as systems; Von B.(1954) defines a system as "an entity which maintains its existence through the mutual interaction of its parts". Harvard Business School (2006) in their book named Systems Thinking Collaborative (2001, p. 1), points out that *"systems thinking provides a necessary conceptual base and a powerful tool-set for working the most complex issues that confront us as individuals or in organization."* One of the strategic area of an organization is the Performance management which clearly indicate the progress of an organization towards its goals by indicating whether they were or not met both effectively or efficiently. This is an important department in building the product/service (McNamara, 1999).

In general strategic thinking is simply a process through which managers synthesize their business environment utilizing both their intuition and creativity for an integrated perspective of the enterprise. Leonidas (2011) adds an aspect of assumptions where leaders take alternative actions within a set of assumptions as well as challenging existing assumptions and action alternatives, potentially leading to new and more appropriate ones. However, system thinking is very interrelated term to strategic thinking since we cannot have a strategy without first understanding the system, yet we cannot have a system without first developing a strategy (Pearl, 2017).

4. Simple and complex systems

The terms Complex and simple are generally used in technical situation referring to the number of components or aspects in a system. Complex system has several elements or several aspects to look out while a simple system is made only with one component. According to the system theory, the complexity of a system does not refer to its difficulty. A system can be complicated but not complex at all (University of Twente, 1990). If a system is complex, it means that it has many components but complexity does not evoke difficulty. While complicated refers to high level of difficulty. On the other hand, Simple system is that with few components and that can be predicted. For instance, if a problem is said complicated when it will certainly take a lot of hard work to solve; complex problem will have many parts while simple problems will involve only one variable.

In business arena, any organization is defined as a system. The difference between simple and complex systems is based on uncertainty/certainty and static/dynamism nature of patterns. Complex business system is the one whose environment has changing trends due to competition, emerging technology, globalization and customer behaviour (Leonidas S, 2011).

Dealing with the above complex systems, requires continuous strategic system thinking and strategic decision making. Organizations may choose to fix some terms and regulations that would guides people's decisions. Though some complex social systems can never be described by a mathematical formula, the distinction between simple and complex systems is the dynamism and certainty. The more we know about system and the better the computational power we use, the more predictable complex systems become.

5. Complex Adaptive Systems
Complex adaptive systems (CAS) are the flexible complex systems that adjust their structures, actions depending on the changing environment. *"Complex adaptive system is a collection of individual agents with freedom to act in ways that are not always totally predictable and whose actions are interconnected so that one agent's actions changes the context for other agents"* (Gplsek and Greenhalgh,2001). An example of adaptive system would be an NGO working in humanitarian sector with an urge to respond to alternative emergency situations   meeting at the same time the donor requirements, working with many other organizations including implementing partners and abiding by the camp regulations such as UNHCR policy.

According to Leonidas S (2011), organizations are described as systems, hence my organization is an adaptive complex system. O, what makes our systems to be complex is the dynamism of our members, the difference in our perspectives, preferences, age, experiences and the individual right for decision making. This is normal for humans as creatures of habit, we often find it difficult to recognize counterproductive patterns of behaviour.

For example my organization is an adaptive complex system. What makes our system to be complex is the dynamism of our members, the difference in our perspectives, preferences, age, experiences and the individual right for decision making. This is normal for us as creatures of habit, we often find it difficult to recognize counterproductive patterns of behaviour. However, it is described as an adaptive system because of its adaptability to work with other many organizations including donors and implementing partners in humanitarian arena.

It is through systematic thinking that managers have to find sustainable solutions to complex problems and offers tools and processes which enable organisations to see patterns and connections, leading to greater productivity. For instance, for our organization to shrive and cope with surrounding and internal challenges, any strategy developed should consider all of these differences and occasional changes within our organization.

6. Practice of a strategy
6.1. Understanding how managers differ in strategizing
According to Jarrat and Stiles (2010), strategy has been academically presented in two models: the process-based model developed through consultation within organization and organizational stakeholders depending on the business environment and an emergent model which (Quinn, 1980) describes as logical incremental, adaptive (Chaffee, 1985) and/or processual (Whittington, 2001). This last model refines the existing organizational strategy depending on environmental context. While the formal strategizing is guided by some traditional structural analysis tools such as SWOT, PEST and BCG (Gunn and Williams, 2007). Bharadwaj, Clark and Kulviwat (2005) have criticized it for of its over-simplificative nature, lack of predictive value and prioritization of factors defined for interrogation with extensions of what is already known. According to Bharadwaj C. and Kulviwat (2005), the emergent "model places less emphasis on the constraints of the firm and historical norms" but rather sees strategizing as a sense-making and pattern matching.

Jarrat and Stiles (2010) point out that, under these two models, there is no preferred practice approach by managers. The selection of strategic tools and how they are used are different since methods and tools are first contextualized in alternative practices in order to be adapted. Here, Jarrat and Stiles adopted the approach of The Vygotsky (1978) and Leontiev (1978) which emphasizes on the practice and sees managers' strategizing as individual process depending on managers' point of views on competitive strategy and the environment. According to Jarrat and stile, it's the activity framework that explains how managers differ in strategizing.

Briefly, there are three strategic practices: firstly there is a routinized practice where managers see their future business environment as expansion of the present environment and hence, predictable. The second practice is a reflective where managers see their business environment as complex and dynamic and strategize accordingly. Lastly, an imposed practice is observed where managers see the business environment as steady and strategy as incremental (Jarrat and Stile (2010).

6.2. Understanding environment in strategic management
Any businesses operates in a changing world and is subject to factors both internal and external which jointly affect its managerial decision-making and which are sometimes beyond their control. Managers are, hence required to scan and understand the impact of their business environment while planning and developing strategies.

As we have seen it above, no business can survive without continued interaction with the internal and external environment. Businesses are usually influenced by forces in their external business and internal environment (Porter, 1980). Porter compares it as a ship at sea, subject to powerful natural forces of which it needs to be aware and deal with. Porter (1980) argues that for any business to navigate its way to success, a business strategy should be developed taking into account all of those forces. This is the only way that opportunities and threats are identified, helping the managers to match internal strengths to external opportunities. Some of the External Business Environment may include Economic, Demographic, Technological, Ecosystem, Political and Legal environment as well as Social/cultural environment. Other factors that are part of an organization's marketing process such as market, its producer/suppliers, and its

7

marketing intermediaries are considered micro-environmental forces but capable of exerting more influence over these than forces in the macro environment (Derric P, 2007). This explains well how systems thinkers should understand the interaction of all those factors.

6.3. Strategic tools for analyzing business Environment
Today's business is much characterized by competition. None of the organizations can survive without the mastery of the environment in which it is operating. In this regard, managers should be well trained for ensuring a good position in their respective industries. Managers should be familiar with various tools used for scanning both the internal and external environment. According to Denise Jarratt and David Stiles (2010) there are various strategic tools for the analyses of the environment. These include the SWOT analysis and the BCG.

SWOT ANALYSIS is a historically popular technique through which managers evaluate the internal **S**trengths and **W**eaknesses of a firm and the environmental **O**pportunities and **T**hreat facing that firm. Using the same tool, managers are able to evaluate internal resources (strengths and weaknesses) as well as its external situation (opportunities and threats). A good business strategy attempts to maximize a firm's strengths and opportunities and minimizes its weaknesses and threats, hence this assumption is also important in designing a successful strategy.

Bolton Consulting Group

This technique, which normally uses the Growth-share matrix, is particularly useful for multi-divisional and/or multiproduct companies. Sabrina and Omar (2013) explains how the divisions or products compromise the organisations business portfolio where the composition of the portfolio can be critical to the growth and success of the company, hence the BCG matrix very supportive analytical tool.

The BCG matrix considers two variables: "**Market growth rate and relative market share.** This Portfolio technique, developed by the **B**oston **C**onsulting **G**roup helps managers to balance the flow of cash resources among their various businesses while also identifying their basic strategic purpose within the overall portfolio (Henderson, 1968)

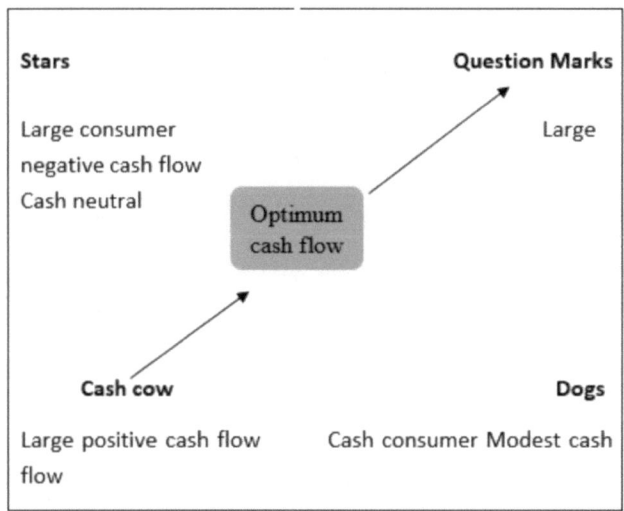

Bolton Consulting Matrix by Henderson (1968)

The four categories represent an increasing/decreasing of market share /market growth rate

Dogs – Status of a business with both low market growth and low market share. Such a business doesn't neither consume much money nor generate income but money invested is tied up in business, hence is candidates for divestiture.

Question marks: Business with high market growth rate but low market share. The result is a large net cash consumption, hence a need to carefully analyze such business in order to determine whether they are worth the

Investment required to grow market share (Business Tools Store, 2013)

Stars: Business with large market share and high growth rate, hence this business generates large amounts of cash but also consumes more cash because of their high growth rate.

Cash cows: Business with high market share and low market growth, hence generating stable cash flow.

The above discussed tools, together with other many tolls, are some of the helpful tools that can help managers to take right strategic decisions when applied appropriately.

6.4. Strategic Change Management

Strategic thinking provides tools for change management, which is an important process through which organizations address actual problems and transition them from the state to the desired future state. The process provides continuous advantages both staffs and their business organizations. Conquest Business Advisors (2015) defines change as a planned and managed process whose benefits are known before implementation and serve as motivators and assessment of progress.

Normally people are left with their culture, usual life practices, understanding, etc. Change would not be thought as a sudden thing. It would require time for people to be trained, convinced and understand. It's just little by little. When people do understand how and why change, we can then stabilize the organization. From this course, I can understand that change should be planed, accessed and communicated to every participant beforehand. Forcing people to implement any change would not be efficient; it is rather better to train them little by little before constitutionalizing the change.

Briefly, I strongly emphasize that when we effectuate a better change management; we can create an efficient communication strategy among employees, we can also easily assess the overall impact of a change, respond faster to customer demands and increase employees contribution when they understand the change process but also with a better change management we can reduce risks associated with our organization

6.5. Strategic Risk Management

By definition, "*risk is an uncertain event that if it occurs, can have a positive or negative effect on a project's goals*" (Vivian, 2016). One of the most important things that mangers should do is to manage these risks on a daily basis. According to Vivian, all risk management processes go through the five basic steps that are: Identification of risk that might affect either our project or its outcomes, risk analysis to know the consequence and impact it may create, ranking the risk depending on its magnitude, risk treatment as well as risk monitoring and review. Business manager should be able to strategically think in a way that addresses anticipated project risks.

Conclusion

Strategic thinking just can't be successfully executed without the right organization design, effective organization design helps build strategic capability. A good strategic design defines clear success indicators and helps the business to be able to adapt changes in the market conditions without negatively affecting employees and suppliers. This implies effective work and refine communication. Trying to find solutions for problems, e.g. in an organisation, by ignoring the fact that the chosen approach will influence many other factors and sub-systems will not help you find a sustainable solution. Systems thinkers will instead have a look at the whole and try to answer the question.

Acknowledgement

This work was carried out as part of the author's learning path at the University of South Wales in the United Kingdom, which is why the author would like to thank the entire academic team for this opportunity and more particularly Prof.Dr. Mike NKASU for his consistent supervision and advice on the project and Leonidas Stergiou, my fellow student who remained closer to inspire and added his incredible contributions.

Bibliography

Ackoff L., R. (2006). Why Few Organizations Adopt Systems Thinking. *Systems Research and Behavioral Science, 23*, 705-708. Retrieved July 21, 2017, from http://onlinelibrary.wiley.com/doi/10.1002/sres.791/abstract

Business Tools store . (2013). Retrieved from BCG Matrix template: http://www.businesstoolsstore.com/bcg-matrix-template-excel/

Conquest Business Advisors. (2015). Retrieved August 05, 2017, from Change management: http://cba.com.cy/wp-content/uploads/Quest_Change_Management.pdf

Derric, P. (2007). Business Environment. Retrieved August 05, 2017, from http://www.gather.com/viewArticle.action?articleId=281474977181396

Feyzollah, & Saeid. (2015). Strategic Thinking and Its Approaches. *Journal of Applied Environmental and Biological Sciences.*

Henderson, B. (1968). *What Is the Growth Share Matrix?* Boston Consulting Group. Retrieved August 15, 2017, from https://www.bcg.com/about/our-history/growth-share-matrix

Jarratt, D., & Stiles, D. (2010). How are methodologies and tools framing managers' strategizing practice in competitive strategy development? *British journal of management.*

Leonidas, S. (2011). Strategic system thinking. Literature review. Retrieved July 23, 2017, from https://www.academia.edu/33637282/Strategic_Systems_Thinking_-_Literature_Review

Ndaruhutse, S., Jones, C., & Riggall, A. (2016). Why systems thinking is important for the education sector. Retrieved from https://files.eric.ed.gov/fulltext/ED603263.pdf

Pearce, J. A., & Robinson, R. B. (2004). *Strategic management: Formulation, implementation, and control (9th ed).* . New York: McGraw-Hill Irwin.

Porter, M. E. (1996). What is Strategy? *Harvard Business Review*, 61-78.

Reisman, R., & Oral, M. (2005). Soft Systems Methodology: A Context within a 50-Year Retrospective of OR/MS. *Interfaces, 35*(2), 164–178. Retrieved July 21, 2017, from http://pubsonline.informs.org/doi/pdf/10.1287/inte.1050.0129

Saad, A. (2013). System Thinking. Retrieved July 27, 2017, from https://www.academia.edu/9568457/System_Thinking

Sabrina, & Omar. (2013). Strategic management, Growth-share matrix. Boston Consulting Group. Retrieved July 23, 2017, from http://www.studymode.com/essays/Boston-Consulting-Group-43875736.html

Stacey, R. (2011). *Strategic management and organizational dynamics: the challenge of complexity* (6 ed.). Harlow: Pearson.

UniversityofTwente. (1990). *System Theory.* Retrieved July 22, 2017, from https://www.utwente.nl/en/bms/communication-theories/sorted-by-cluster/Communication%20Processes/System_Theory/

Vivian, K. (2016). What are the 5 risk management steps in a sound risk management process? Retrieved July 23, 2017, from http://continuingprofessionaldevelopment.org/risk-management-steps-in-risk-management-process/?

Zhu, P. (2017). System thinking Vs Strategic thinking. Retrieved July 23, 2017, from http://futureofcio.blogspot.com/2014/06/system-thinking-vs-strategic-thinking.html

YOUR KNOWLEDGE HAS VALUE

- We will publish your bachelor's and
  master's thesis, essays and papers

- Your own eBook and book -
  sold worldwide in all relevant shops

- Earn money with each sale

Upload your text at www.GRIN.com
and publish for free